RASCALLY RABBITS!

And More True Stories of Animals Behaving Badly!

Aline Alexander Newman

NATIONAL GEOGRAPHIC

SCHOLASTIC INC.

ISBN 978-1-338-03566-7

12 11 10 9 8 7 6 5 4 3 2   16 17 18 19 20 21

Printed in the U.S.A.   40

First Scholastic printing, March 2016

Staff for This Book
Shelby Alinsky, *Project Editor*
Callie Broaddus, *Art Director*
Ruth Ann Thompson, *Designer*
Bri Bertoia, *Photo Editor*
Marfé Ferguson Delano, *Editor*
Paige Towler, *Editorial Assistant*
Rachel Kenny and Sanjida Rashid, *Design Production Assistants*
Tammi Colleary-Loach, *Rights Clearance Manager*
Michael Cassady and Mari Robinson, *Rights Clearance Specialists*

Table of
CONTENTS

SNIFFLES AND BABBITY: RASCALLY RABBITS

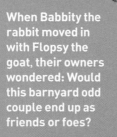

When Babbity the rabbit moved in with Flopsy the goat, their owners wondered: Would this barnyard odd couple end up as friends or foes?

Sweet little Sniffles has soft fur, stiff ears, big eyes, and a supersize sneaky streak.

Chapter 1

SNEAKY SNIFFLES

Wade Newman had no time to waste. Night was falling in Turin, New York, U.S.A. And his rabbit, Sniffles, was missing. The 14-year-old boy had to find the little bunny before the evening turned too dark to see.

Wade searched his yard. He peered under bushes and poked into weeds. He looked behind the garage and on top of the woodpile. But snuggly Sniffles was nowhere to be found.

Earlier that afternoon, Wade had let the rabbit out of its hutch. His dog, Boo Boo, was running loose in the yard. So was Sparky the cat. *Sniffles needs to have his own adventure,* Wade thought.

It seemed safe enough. Wade lived in dairy-farming country. His family's house sat far back from the road. A creek ran along one side and a large cornfield bordered the other. Out back stretched a rocky cow pasture.

The only trouble was Sniffles' small size. He was a Netherland (sounds like NETH-er-land) dwarf rabbit and weighed just two pounds (0.9 kg). The little hopper could disappear in tall grass or hide inside a flower pot. *So where is he now?* Wade wondered. *I've always been able to find him before.*

Never once had he let Sniffles or Boo Boo stay outside all night. Sparky did sometimes stay out. Like all cats, Sparky had excellent night vision and enjoyed prowling in the dark.

If only I could see that well, wished Wade. But he couldn't. When total darkness fell, he gave up looking for Sniffles.

Scary thoughts rushed through Wade's mind when he tried to sleep. *Was Sniffles lost? Had he been nabbed by an owl or coyote?* If only the rabbit had stayed in sight.

Big Bunnies, Little Bunnies

From forests to deserts, rabbits live all over the world. People began taming them about 500 years ago. Today there are 48 breeds, or kinds, of tame rabbits. The breeds differ in color, looks, and type of fur.

But breed doesn't affect how friendly a bunny will be. So when choosing a pet, think about size. There are tiny, 3-pound (1.4 kg) "pocket pets" like the lionhead (shown here). And there are 20-pound (9.0 kg) checkered giants. Pick the bunny that you have room for, can afford to feed, and find easy to handle.

Morning finally came, and Wade's father found Sparky sitting on the back porch stoop. And, surprise! Beside him sat Sniffles! *How did that happen?* Wade wondered. *Were Sparky and Sniffles together all night? Or did they meet up at dawn?*

Wade would never know. But relief flooded over him as he scooped up his bunny and rubbed him against his cheek.

Sniffles had returned unharmed, so Wade continued to let him out of his hutch. "Don't go far, and come back before dark," he told the bunny. But did Sniffles listen? No! The naughty bunny missed curfew many times. Wade learned not to worry and just wait until morning. Then Sniffles and Sparky would appear at the door.

But Sparky was old, and he eventually

died. Everyone missed him, including Sniffles. The bunny had lost his friend and his guide. Wade worried that without Sparky, Sniffles might not find his way home. So Wade stopped letting the rabbit loose in the yard. He began bringing him inside the house instead.

Wade usually did this at night, when he lay on the couch and watched TV. Then Sniffles would crawl inside one of Wade's pants' pockets and sleep.

One night, Wade was focused on his TV show. He failed to notice when the little rabbit started chewing. Chewing is a natural behavior for rabbits. So doing it must have felt good to Sniffles. But he nibbled a big hole in Wade's best pants. Oops!

Other problems came up. Hopping around outside used to wear down Sniffles' nails. Now that he no longer did that, his nails grew too long. Wade's mom tried to cut them. But Sniffles wriggled and squirmed. Once she cut too deep by mistake, and it made the rabbit's toe bleed.

Sniffles was acting different, too. He used to show joy by jumping straight up and to the side. But the bunny stopped doing his happy dance.

Wade hated to see Sniffles so sad. So he took a risk. He started letting Sniffles run loose outdoors again.

All went well for a while. Then one day Sniffles disappeared and did not return. Wade felt terrible. *Is my funny bunny lost for good?* he wondered. *If only Sparky was still alive.*

Wade and his parents were outside searching for the little rabbit when Boo Boo joined them. That gave Wade an idea. Specially trained search-and-rescue dogs found missing people. Could his untrained mutt find a missing rabbit? It was worth a try. "Boo," he said. "Go find the rabbit."

To his surprise, the dog seemed to understand. Boo Boo immediately put her nose to the ground. She zigged and zagged. Then she picked up speed. "She's got it!" Wade's dad said. "Boo Boo has picked up Sniffles' scent."

The dog headed straight for the neighbor's cornfield. Time passed. Wade grew concerned and plunged into the corn himself. Then he saw them! Boo Boo was walking behind Sniffles and pushing him along with her nose. Every time Sniffles stopped moving, Boo Boo nudged him again. "Good ole Boo," said Wade, amazed. "Thank you for nosing Sniffles home!"

Boo Boo found Sniffles many times after that. Once, the rabbit was lost for so long that everyone had given up hope. Everyone but Boo, that is. On day four, a neighbor called. Boo Boo had found Sniffles inside the neighbor's garage. Wade rushed right over and got both pets.

Thanks to his animal friends, Sniffles enjoyed a long and happy life. He lived for nine years. That is old for a bunny, especially a misbehaving bunny with a lousy sense of direction.

Babbity the rabbit and Flopsy the goat check each other out, while Flopsy's kids nibble hay.

Chapter 2

BABBITY BREAKS OUT

About 450 miles (724 km) south of Sniffles and Wade's home lived another bunny with a taste for adventure. But you wouldn't know it to look at him. The big, black bunny huddled alone in a corner of his cage. His busy owners fed him every day. They cleaned his cage and kept his water bottle full. But that was all. The sad-looking bunny had no toys and no rabbit friends. He had not been out of his cage in two long years.

Finley Broaddus (sounds like FINN-lee BRAH-dus) and her family lived on the farm next door. It was an "Old MacDonald" type of farm called Tranquility (sounds like tran-KWIL-ih-tee) Post, in Warrenton, Virginia, U.S.A. And on this farm, they had 3 horses, 3 Nigerian (sounds like nigh-JEER-ee-un) dwarf goats, 25 chickens, 2 cats, and 1 dog. Finley's family kept enough different kinds of pets to sing five verses of "Finley Broaddus had a farm. *EE-I-EE-I-O.*"

But they didn't have any rabbits. And 16-year-old Finley and her sister, Callie, loved rabbits. Finley often thought about their neighbor's rabbit. She saw it every day. Its cage stood next to the Tranquility Post fence. Seeing the rabbit all alone out there always brought a lump to Finley's throat. *Poor bunny,* she thought. *You lead such a lonely life. Nobody pays any attention to you.*

Finley knew her neighbors well. She sometimes babysat for their three youngest boys. So one day she gathered her courage. "I like your rabbit," she said. "May I have him?"

Did You Know?

Rabbits whose ears hang down the sides of their head are called lop-eared.

"Yes!" said her neighbors. They were happy to find him a good home.

Finley and her dad set to work fixing up their old rabbit hutch. Her dad had built the hutch years before. It was a big, wooden box standing on legs. Inside were two rooms. The walls of the larger room were made of wire mesh. A climbing shelf was mounted on one wall. And a mesh "skylight" let in the sun.

The smaller room was like a closet. It was snug and dark like a wild rabbit's burrow. That served as the bunny's hideout.

Finley cleaned out the hutch and hosed it down. Then her dad replaced the old shingle roof with a new metal one. They also mended holes in the wire mesh.

Finley hung a plastic water bottle in the hutch. She added a food dish, salt wheel, birdseed cake, and a chew toy. Without something to chew, her rabbit's front teeth would grow long and curved like walrus tusks.

How to Hold a Pet Rabbit

Many animals hunt rabbits for food. So it's no wonder rabbits are fearful by nature. That's why it's important to be very gentle when you handle one. Before you pick up a bunny, let it sniff your hand. Calm it by speaking gently.

Lift the rabbit with both hands. Put one hand under its chest. Support its rump with the other. Hold the rabbit firmly against your stomach. Never lift a bunny by the scruff of its neck or by its ears. Bunnies have sensitive ears, and they hate hanging in the air.

Now the hutch was ready. Finley went to get the bunny from her neighbors. But when she opened the cage door, the rabbit panicked. His eyes looked ready to pop out of his head. He flattened his ears and braced himself against one wall. The bunny's whole body screamed "Stay away!" What a struggle! Using two hands, Finley finally managed to turn the rabbit around. Then she gently pulled him out tail first.

"Everything will be okay," she whispered. "I am giving you a new home and a new name. We will call you Babbity Rabbity." Babbity Rabbity was a character in the Harry Potter books. The fearful bunny pumped his hind legs. He tried to get away. But Finley held her furry bundle close and carried him home.

Babbity's new home was in the goat paddock (sounds like PAD-ock). The paddock was a small field surrounded by a wooden fence. The fence was covered with wire mesh.

Besides the rabbit hutch, a small goat house stood in the paddock. The goats went inside the house to get out of the sun. It also sheltered them from wind and rain. A wooden platform under the roof served as their bed.

Finley opened the hutch door and tucked Babbity inside. "I hope you like it here," she told him. "I'll come back tomorrow and let you out. Then you can stretch your legs."

Finley and Callie both cared for the bunny. They fed him carrots from the garden. Chomp! Chomp! And they gave him the dandelions that grew by the barn. Nibble. Nibble. Mostly they petted and held him. They wanted Babbity to feel safe around people.

In nice weather, the sisters moved the goats into a larger pasture. Then they let Babbity run loose in the paddock. The rabbit was so happy he jumped for joy! He hopped around the paddock. He explored the goat house. And he gobbled up the fresh green grass. After an hour, the girls put Babbity back in his cage. But watching him had given Finley an idea. *What if we cut a hole in the floor of his hutch and build a ramp to the ground?* she thought. *Then Babbity could come and go as he pleases.*

Finley's dad liked that idea. He sawed the hole and built a ramp like Finley wanted. But then he worried. Suppose Babbity got out when the goats were around? They might trample the clueless bunny! So Finley's dad cut a square of wire mesh and framed it with wood. This created a sort of trap door. Finley and Callie used that to cover the hole when the goats were in the paddock.

But Babbity had spent too many years living a lonely life. He wanted company. One morning, Finley walked into the paddock to feed the animals. And what did she see on the grass? "Babbity!" she cried. "How did you get out?"

Flopsy better eat fast! Greedy Babbity is eyeing her breakfast, and what Babbity wants, Babbity usually gets.

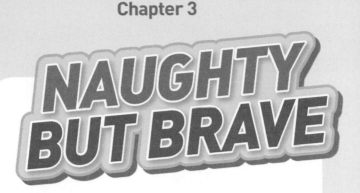

Chapter 3

NAUGHTY BUT BRAVE

Clever Babbity must have dragged the trap door aside with his teeth. Now he was hopping with the goats! Finley caught him and popped him back in the hutch.

The next day, Callie fed the animals. She was pouring grain into the feed bucket for Flopsy, the mama goat, when Babbity appeared again. Uh-oh.

Flopsy stared hard at the nervy bunny. Did he want her breakfast? The mama goat laid back her ears. "Flopsy, no!" yelled Callie. But the angry goat charged. She flung her head. Bam! The battered bunny flew through the air. Thump! He crash-landed in the dirt.

Callie gasped. *Was Babbity hurt?* She ran to help him. But the gutsy fur ball jumped to his feet. Like a fighter in the ring, he went back for more. Again and again, Flopsy head-butted the pesky rabbit. But he refused to quit. The barnyard rivals battled it out for weeks.

And the winner was … Babbity!

Callie and Finley were surprised. The rabbit acted shy with them. Yet he was fearless around the goats. And once the fighting ended, Babbity and Flopsy became friends.

First, the rabbit sniffed Flopsy's ears while she ate. Then he dared to hang over the rim of her bucket. That way he could reach the grain, too. Yummy!

For a while, goat and rabbit ate head to head. But Flopsy finally gave up! She let Babbity eat from her bucket all by himself. Then she and her two kids fought over the other two pails.

From then on, Babbity never returned to his hutch. He ate, drank, and slept with the goats.

Then one day, somebody forgot to shut the paddock door. When Callie went to do chores, she found an open gate and the goats in the pasture. *Oh, no! Babbity!* she thought. Callie ran into the paddock. She searched the goat house and the rabbit hutch. Babbity had escaped!

Meanwhile, the horses had spotted Callie walking down the driveway. Feeding time! They nickered loudly and galloped back toward the barn. The goats heard them and lifted their heads. They sprinted back to their paddock.

Despite being worried about Babbity, Callie had to feed the other animals. The goats circled her as she poured their grain. They brushed against her legs and head-butted her bucket. "Calm down!" she said. "You'll get your share." But sad thoughts swirled in her brain. *Babbity is missing.*

Callie raised her eyes and glanced out

over the pasture. The sun was setting, and it would soon be too dark to hunt for the bunny. Callie's heart sank. Then she spotted a black speck in the sea of green grass. The longer Callie watched, the bigger the speck grew. Could it be Babbity? Yes! Babbity was coming!

From then on, life in the barnyard was like that old nursery rhyme. Only, at Tranquility Post, Mary didn't have a little lamb. Flopsy had a little bunny. And everywhere that Flopsy went, the bunny was sure to go. When the goats went into the bigger pasture, Babbity followed them. When the younger goats climbed on a pile of logs, Flopsy gobbled up leafy green plants growing along the fence line. And Babbity sat beside Flopsy, sniffing her feet.

Stinky? Sure. But the mama goat's familiar smell comforted the rabbit. When the goats stayed out all night, so did Babbity.

Beyond the pasture lay a large woodland. It was full of foxes, raccoons, eagles, and hawks—all of which liked rabbit for supper. Callie and Finley worried when Babbity stayed out at night. But every morning, they found him sitting with the goats, hungry for breakfast.

One day, Callie was cleaning out the goat pen when she heard, *eh-eh-a-oooo!* Turning around, she saw Buddy the rooster—with his claws raised!

Callie staggered backward. *If only Finley was here,* she thought. *Buddy never attacks her. She could catch him so I could escape.* Without Finley to help, Callie had

Did You Know?

A male rabbit is called a buck. Females are called does, and babies are kits.

to kick Buddy to drive him away. And the minute she did, Flopsy came running. *Bam!* She head-butted Callie's other leg. *What was that for?* Callie wondered. Then she remembered. Flopsy liked Buddy. And Flopsy protected her friends. *So that's it,* Callie thought. *Flopsy protects Babbity at night.*

Callie looked at the rabbit and smiled. She and Finley had laughed about it so many times. The bunny looked so small and helpless. Yet the rascally rabbit was boss of the barnyard, the supreme ruler. There he was, stretched out on top of the hay, while all three goats nibbled happily around him. They would never even think of butting him away.

Baby Boom

The word "tranquility" means peace, or calm. But life at Tranquility Post was far from calm with Babbity around. The craziness continued when Callie and Finley rescued two more bunnies. Quite by accident, boy met girl. And guess what?

Babies! They were born bald. But two weeks later, they looked like balls of fluff. Callie moved the boys, Bugs and Inky, into an empty horse stall. She put the girl bunnies into another stall. But the old barn had a dirt floor.

One day, Bugs (the bunny on the cover) started digging. He didn't stop until he reached the goat pen. Inky (shown here) followed him through the tunnel. Then the young bunnies sneaked across the paddock

and squeezed
through the fence.
Somehow they made
it to the front yard.

Unlike Babbity, Inky and
Bugs didn't have Flopsy around to protect
them. But lucky for them, Mrs. Broaddus
spotted them before a hungry hawk or fox
did. "The bunnies are out!" she cried. The
family came to the rescue. For over an
hour, they chased after the bunnies,
waggling carrots.

"Whew," sighed Callie, once the
rascals were rounded up. "It's a good
thing they didn't tunnel into the girl
bunnies' stall. That could have led to even
more babies and more commotion!"

Got any marshmallows? Tempted by an easy-to-open cooler full of tasty treats, a hungry bear raids a campsite.

YELLOW-YELLOW: BANDIT BEAR

Standing tall, a black bear takes a break from clawing a tree. Could it be smelling food nearby?

It was summer in the Adirondack (sounds like ad-ih-RON-dack) Park in New York State, U.S.A. A group of hikers were climbing Mount Marcy, the park's tallest peak. Along the way, they set up camp in a lean-to, or three-sided shelter, beside the trail. They shed their backpacks and ate. Then they sat down to rest.

Meanwhile, a female black bear

was hiding in the woods. Her nose quivered as she smelled the campers' tasty feast. She wanted what they were eating, but she stayed quiet and waited. Once the hikers were still—zoom! The bear dashed out from behind a tree. She knew backpacks often held food, so she grabbed one with her teeth. "Hey! Hey!" the startled campers yelled. But the furry thief quickly dragged the backpack away.

The crook was easy to describe. She was small and had one yellow ear tag.

Ben Tabor knew that outlaw well. People called her Yellow-Yellow, because she once had two yellow ear tags—one in each ear. But somehow one of her tags had come off. Ben is a wildlife biologist, a scientist who studies animals. He works for the New York State Department of Environmental (sounds like in-vi-run-MENT-ul) Conservation, or DEC. Ben's beat is the Adirondack High Peaks, where Mount Marcy draws over 110,000 visitors each year. "So many people bring in so much food," Ben said. "That makes it easy for bears to get in trouble."

Over the years, cautious (sounds like CAW-shus) campers had tried to outwit the bears. They hung their packs from cables strung between two trees. But the bears climbed the trees, crossed the cables, and stole the food.

Other campers were careless. They didn't clean up after meals, or they stored snacks inside their tents. This tempted the bears.

A few campers even fed bears on purpose! They wanted to see wild animals up close. But easy access to people food made the bears want more and more of it. They entered tents and bullied campers.

People got mad when bears stole their grub. In 2004 alone, the DEC received 480 bear complaints. Something had to be done. So the DEC hired Ben to study the bears and find a way for campers and bears to live in peace.

First Ben had to trap the bears and record their age, gender, and size. Then he would give each one ear tags and a tracking collar. People could identify the crooks by the color of their tags. And Ben would know where each bear went. Over time, he'd learn which bears caused the most trouble.

Hungry, Hungry Bears

Bears are eating machines. They stuff themselves during the warm months. Then they snooze all winter without eating a thing. They live off their body fat.

Much of the food bears eat is tiny. They spend days plucking blueberries or raspberries one at a time, with their lips. Imagine a 400-pound (181-kg) bear trying to fill up on ants or honeybees! That's a lot of work. And bears do get stung. No wonder they go for people food, if it's easy to get!

Come fall, apples, cherries, acorns, and beechnuts get ripe. That's when bears can really pack on the pounds.

It's not easy to trap a bear. The trickiest part is figuring out where a bear might be. Then you have to hide your own scent. One whiff of a human would make many bears run away. So Ben had to boil all the parts of the trap and seal them in plastic beforehand. He wore rubber gloves while putting the parts together.

Ben was helped by Lou Berchelli (sounds like bur-CHEL-ee), another bear biologist. The two scientists hoped they could catch Yellow-Yellow. Lou had trapped her a few years earlier. He had attached the yellow tags that gave the bear her name. Now he thought she might be the main robber.

In August 2004, the men set a trap on a known bear trail. The trap looked like a hole in the ground. But there was a ring of cable around its rim and a foot pedal in the bottom. The cable was hooked to a nearby tree.

Normally Ben would never feed a bear human food. But the best way to catch a potential robber was with a sweet treat. So he dumped some doughnuts into the trap. He covered them with moss, and he and Lou left. They would check back often.

Sniff, sniff. A smallish bear found the goodies. When she tried to paw them out of the hole, she pushed the pedal. *Sproing!* The cable snared her leg. It didn't hurt, but it tied her to the tree.

"Looks like we caught Yellow-Yellow!" Ben said when he saw the trapped bear's ear tags. He shot a drug-filled dart into her. The drug made her unable to move for a while, but she could hear and see. Ben blindfolded her to keep her calm.

The scientists rolled the bear into a canvas cradle hooked to spring scales. They hung the scales on a sawed-off tree branch and heaved the branch up on their shoulders. The bear weighed a healthy 120 pounds (54 kg).

Yellow-Yellow would never miss one small back tooth. So Ben pulled one to send to the lab. Viewing a slice of its root under the microscope would reveal her age. Ben also snipped a clump of her hair. Chemicals found there would show if she had been eating human food.

Finally, Ben put a collar around the

bear's neck. It had a battery-operated GPS unit on it that would track her movements. This collar cost a fortune. But Ben could download data from it to his computer. "Now I will know everywhere you go," he told Yellow-Yellow. "So behave yourself."

Ben removed her blindfold. Once she could run again, he shot her in the behind with rubber pellets. Ouch! It didn't harm her, but Ben hoped that little "spanking" would make her want to avoid people.

A few days later, Ben heard from the lab. Yellow-Yellow was 11 years old. And yes, she had been eating human food.

Ben mapped Yellow-Yellow's travels until fall. Then, uh-oh. His GPS receiver started beeping fast. That meant either the bear's collar had fallen off—or she had died.

After blindfolding her, wildlife biologists Ed Reed (left) and Benjamin P. Tabor put a GPS collar on Yellow-Yellow. Behind them is the trap they used to catch the bear.

Chapter 2

CATCH HER IF YOU CAN

The next day, Ben and a crew climbed Mount Marcy. They headed for Yellow-Yellow's last known location, a grove of cherry trees. Ben wore the GPS receiver around his neck and held an antenna over his head. Up on the ridge, he turned in a circle, letting the antenna search the sky. When it picked up a radio signal coming from the collar, the receiver beeped. The beeps got softer when he walked the wrong way. They sounded louder when he got closer.

Everyone searched the area. Then Ben spied a hopeful sign—bear poop! You might hold your nose. But Ben was thrilled. He craned his neck and looked up. Yes! A wide, leather collar dangled from a broken tree branch. Yellow-Yellow must have climbed the tree and snagged her collar while climbing down.

Whew! Yellow-Yellow was probably fine. Ben scampered up the tree after the costly collar.

The only trouble now was that he couldn't track the bear. And he

Did You Know?

An adult female bear is called a sow or she-bear. An adult male bear is called a boar.

couldn't put the collar back on her, because he couldn't find her. She had probably curled up in her den for the winter. Ben sighed. He was playing hide-and-seek with a bear. And the bear was winning!

To be sure of catching Yellow-Yellow in the spring, Ben planned to set more than one trap. He would use leg snares and a culvert trap. The culvert trap looked like a big, green barrel lying on its side. It had a window in one end and a drop-down door in the other.

And it was heavy. No way could Ben lug that up the mountain. Nor could he drive his truck on the rugged woodland trail. For this job, Ben needed a helicopter!

The helicopter had a long cable hanging from its belly. The cable was attached to a big canvas sling. Ben strapped the sling around the trap. The chopper whirred and lifted up. Then away it flew. The trap dangled in the air like an unwound yo-yo.

The pilot set the trap down in a snow-covered raspberry patch behind Marcy Dam. Ben had seen shredded backpacks there. So he knew bears used the spot. But they wouldn't use it again until summer, when the tourists arrived.

Finally, one warm June day, Ben hiked up to the dam. He set up the leg snares and propped open the door to the culvert trap. He baited all the traps with doughnuts. Then he mounted a video camera nearby and left.

The yummy doughnut smell floated on the wind, and soon Yellow-Yellow appeared. She wandered around, sniffing the air. She stood on her hind feet and looked for danger. But, in the end, she entered the barrel. Her foot tripped the wire that held up the door, and clang! Down it dropped.

Ben saw her on the video and came back. This time he fitted a drug-filled syringe (sounds like suh-RINJ) into the end of a long pole. Then he poked the pole through the trap window and stuck the doughnut thief in the rump. Yellow-Yellow slumped over, unable to move.

Ben and a helper dragged the bear out of the trap. Ben covered her eyes. Then he slid the GPS collar over her head and checked the fit. Once the bear could run again, he planned to "spank" her with rubber pellets, like before. But Yellow-Yellow pulled a fast one. After Ben removed her blindfold and the drug wore off, she crawled away. When she reached the bushes, zoom! She bolted. Ben laughed. *What a sneak!* he thought.

Ben started tracking Yellow-Yellow again. But two months later the signals from her collar grew weak. *I'd better catch her and replace the batteries,* he thought. He hiked back up to Marcy Dam and reset the culvert trap in the berry patch. Again, he mounted a video camera nearby. For all Ben knew, the clever little bear was hiding somewhere watching him do it.

Soon the camera caught Yellow-Yellow walking past the trap. Like a good little bear, she was still wearing her collar.

Great! Ben thought. *We're in luck.*

But Yellow-Yellow did not enter the trap that night. Or the next. For two days Ben waited. Finally, on day three, Yellow-Yellow's sweet tooth won out. She entered the trap to get the doughnuts. Clang!

Ben rushed out to switch the batteries in the collar. But when he peered through the trap window, *aaarrgh!* Yellow-Yellow's neck was bare. In the two days before getting caught, she had slipped her collar. Again! And now its batteries were dead. So the $4,200 collar was lost forever!

Ben drugged the bear again. This time he put a cheap radio collar on her. It was less accurate, but it was all he had left.

Ben knew it was silly, but he couldn't help wondering. *Does Yellow-Yellow keep losing collars by accident? Or is this sly bear just messing with me?*

Meanwhile, a California engineer named Jamie Hogan had invented a food holder for campers. He called it the BearVault. The BearVault worked like a childproof medicine bottle. You had to push and hold in a button while twisting off the cap. Black bears in California's Folsom City Zoo could not break into it. Nor could the superstrong 1,000-pound (453-kg) grizzly bears in Yellowstone National Park. The BearVault was so hard to open that some humans could not do it. It was the perfect way to stop bear thieves. Or was it?

Bear Can Basics

BearVaults and other bear cans are hard plastic storage containers designed to keep food safe from bears. But for a bear can to work, you must pack all your food inside it. Then you should put in anything else that has an odor. This includes toothpaste, sunblock, even garbage. Garbage smells like food to bears!

Store the bear can at least 100 feet (30 m) from where you sleep. Always remember to properly close the lid. And don't put it on a cliff or beside a stream. A bear might swat it over the edge or into the water!

Mmmm! A bear munches a snack it doesn't have to steal: bright yellow dandelion flowers.

Chapter 3

IN THE SPOTLIGHT

Food! That caused almost all of the troubles between humans and bears. So in 2005, the DEC made a new rule. They said that campers in the Adirondack High Peaks must store their grub in bear cans, such as BearVaults.

This helped for a little while. Then campers using BearVaults began having problems. A bear was breaking into them! Can you guess which bear it was?

If you guessed the BearVault bandit was Yellow-Yellow, you're right. Her radio collar showed that she had been in the area during most of the thefts.

One time Ben saw the sneak in action. He spotted her poking around a pile of BearVaults at a campsite. The campers had gone somewhere and left the cans behind. Ben watched through binoculars as Yellow-Yellow rolled one with her paw. Then she pushed the button and turned the lid with her teeth. Pop! She pulled off the lid, grabbed the picnic, and ran. "Wow! It only took her seconds," said Ben.

Jamie Hogan, the BearVault inventor, heard the news and went right to work.

In 2008, he brought out a new model. This can had two buttons instead of one. And it worked well—too well. Some people found it so hard to remove the tops that they only put them on part way.

Ben thought that was why Yellow-Yellow could open this new model, too. She must have found a can with a loose lid. That was how she pulled it off.

Jamie Hogan agreed that the bear probably got lucky at first. But he thought there was more to it. Over time, Yellow-Yellow opened many of the BearVaults. Jamie collected some of them and studied her tooth marks. "She figured it out," he

Did You Know?

Bears are creatures of habit. They walk the same trails over and over.

said. "She knew what to look for. Over six weeks, she went from attacking the whole lid to biting just the bumps."

Yellow-Yellow had hit the jackpot! Forget plucking berries one by one. Now she could pig out on pork chops, cheese, and trail mix. Yum!

Rangers posted signs warning campers not to use BearVaults. They said to use another kind of bear can instead.

Then a newspaper reporter from the *New York Times* heard about the bear burglar. She interviewed Jamie Hogan. He said BearVaults worked fine in every other park all over the United States. Only in the High Peaks was there a problem. The reason why was Yellow-Yellow. He called her a "genius bear."

Shoo, Bear! Don't Bother Me

Black bears almost never attack people. You are 350 times more likely to be killed by lightning than by a black bear. But suppose "Teddy" comes too close. Experts say you should stay calm and speak softly. Slowly back away, giving the bear an escape route.

If the bear charges, be brave and stand still. It will probably stop or turn away. Do NOT run! Nobody can outrun a bear. Instead, shout and make noise. Wave your arms or throw something at it. If the bear touches you, punch it in the nose. That should send it packing.

And that did it! Thousands of people read that article. Campers flocked to Mount Marcy, looking for the "genius bear." Some even set out food to lure her to their site.

This upset Ben. The campers were teaching Yellow-Yellow bad habits. And unfair as it was, the bears always paid for people's mistakes. Plus, calling Yellow-Yellow a genius made people think she was the only bear that could open the cans. "We know at least three bears that can open those canisters," Ben said.

One night, one of those other bears surprised some humans. A father and son were sleeping in a lean-to. Suddenly a huge male bear with red and green ear tags lumbered in. He only wanted supper, but

Did You Know?

Most mama bears have twins, but really fat bears can have litters of six.

to the people, he seemed dangerous.

The people yelled. He didn't leave. They threw things. He didn't leave. As a last resort, they swatted him with their hiking sticks. That finally drove him away. Later, the father and son reported the clash.

Run-ins with humans land bears in big trouble. The DEC could not move Red-Green to another area, because he'd find his way back. No zoo could take him in. Even though the bear hadn't hurt anyone, the DEC had no choice. Human safety comes first. They hated doing it, but the rangers had to put Red-Green down so he couldn't be a danger to humans.

Ben worried. Would Yellow-Yellow meet the same sad end as Red-Green?

Being famous put her at high risk. Visitors blamed her for everything. Some people claimed she taught her cubs her tricks.

But Ben denied that. He said all bears learn by trial and error. Since Mount Marcy draws more backpackers than other places, bears living there had more chances to learn.

Still, Yellow-Yellow's legend kept growing. Some people thought the park should do away with her. But Ben refused. "Yellow-Yellow is not a bully," he said. "She is a good bear. She keeps bolder bears away."

Soon campers began storing food in different bear cans. And they kept the cans tightly closed. As a result, the number of problem bear complaints in the

Adirondack High Peaks dropped greatly. It went from 480 in 2004 to only 24 in 2013. And that's not all. Ben says that the park rangers have not had to put down a bear on Mount Marcy since Red-Green.

Once people food became hard to get, Yellow-Yellow had to eat more natural food. Bye-bye candy bars, hello acorns. She lived to be 19 years old, which is an old age for a wild bear. Ben felt sad when she died. But he knew that she had enjoyed a good life.

Today, Yellow-Yellow's collar sits on a bookcase in Ben's office. It reminds him of the crafty little bandit bear that forced campers to change their ways. She did that by stealing their food. But in the process, she also managed to steal his heart.

Running so fast that his ears stand on end, Moose bounds across the lawn. He is always ready for adventure.

MOOSE: PROBLEM PUP

Moose may look innocent, but don't be fooled by his charm. Behind those soft, brown eyes lurks a busy brain devoted to mischief and pranks.

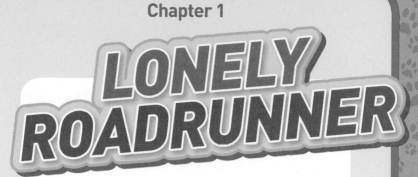

LONELY ROADRUNNER

A young black dog ran without purpose along a forest road in Lewis County, New York, U.S.A. Rain was pouring down and freezing on the ground. Tiny icicles hung from the dog's ears and chin. He had a wild-eyed look on his face.

There were no houses on that part of the Moose River Road. The pitiful puppy had nowhere to go—and no one, it seemed, who cared.

Toward dark, a green minivan drove around the bend. Neil and Aline Newman were heading home to Turin, New York. It was late November. They had spent the day clearing leaves off the roof of their camp, or summer home, in the Adirondack Mountains. They were ready to relax. They did not expect to stumble upon an abandoned pup.

"Stop!" yelled Aline. "There's a dog in the road!"

Neil slammed on the brakes. "What's he doing here?"

"He's not wearing a collar. Maybe he scooted out an open door and got lost," said his wife. "We've got to catch him."

Neil pulled off the road and parked.

Aline buttoned her coat and stepped out into the rain. "Here, puppy," she called, walking slowly toward the dog. "Come." But the dog stiffened and showed the whites of his eyes. He looked ready to bolt.

Neil stood beside the road watching for traffic. He did not want the dog to get hit by a car.

Aline returned to the van. *If only I had a fishy-smelling tuna sandwich for him to sniff,* she thought. But all she found were crackers. She held one out and approached the frightened dog again. "Come, boy," she said, keeping her voice calm.

The dog stared at the food with hungry

Did You Know?

Scientists say that when people gaze into their dog's eyes, it promotes a loving feeling in both the dog and its owner.

eyes. But his body trembled with fear. Finally, he tucked his tail, dropped down to the ground, and crawled on his belly. Each time he moved closer, Aline inched backward. Crawl. Inch. Crawl. Inch. It seemed to take forever. When Aline reached the van, she crouched down. The dog stretched his neck. Gulp! He swallowed the cracker whole.

Now the pup wanted more. He sat up and cautiously raised one paw. Aline knew this was dog speak for "Please don't hurt me. I'll do anything you want."

The pounding rain made it hard to see. Aline took cover in the back seat of the van. She tried to make the dog follow by handing him crackers through the open door. He would start to come, but lose his nerve. Aline only had one cracker left when the pooch gathered his courage. He leaped onto the backseat beside her. Hurrah! Neil ran over and slid the door shut.

This was a dangerous moment. Some dogs would realize they were trapped and panic. They might attack.

But not this dog. This dog shook all over to calm himself. Then he sighed, and his muscles relaxed like melted ice cream.

Aline reached out to pet the pup, as Neil turned the van toward home.

That same night, the Newmans took the dog to the veterinarian (sounds like vet-er-ih-NAIR-ee-en), or vet. Dr. Deanna Fuller checked him for a microchip. Sadly, this pup did not have one. She looked at his teeth and guessed he was about ten months old. Then she weighed him. Yikes! Eighty pounds (36 kg) and still growing!

Aline posted the dog's picture on Facebook. She advertised him on the radio. And she reported him to animal control. Days passed. No one claimed the mutt. *Now what?* she wondered.

Aline had recently told one of her sons that she wanted a dog. Then this dog appeared. Aline believed the pup was meant for her, and she wanted to adopt him.

But Neil was still sad about the death of their last dog. He was not ready for another. Worse yet, he had a bad feeling about this one. "We can't keep him," he said. "The dog is too big for us. I'm afraid he could hurt someone."

Protect Your Pooch

A vet scans a dog for a microchip.

In April 2014, a dog named Gidget disappeared from her home in Pennsylvania, U.S.A. Her owners thought she had gotten lost or been stolen. But five months later she turned up at an animal shelter in Oregon—3,000 miles (4,828 km) away!

Gidget was lucky. She had a microchip under her skin. This tiny device contains an ID number. A shelter worker waved a scanner over Gidget's back, and it read the chip. The ID number led to the pup's owners.

Any vet can microchip your pet. It's cheap, painless, and worth doing. Just ask Gidget!

Yet even Neil liked the silly mutt. The dog rarely barked. And he was perfectly housebroken. He rattled the doorknob with his nose when he wanted to go out, or he brought them his leash. In fact, the pooch was so friendly and lovable that, after a few days, he won Neil over. "I give in," Neil told Aline. "The dog can stay."

Did You Know?

In Spain, by law all dogs must have microchips.

Neil and Aline named the mutt Moose, after the road where they found him. They bought him a comfy dog bed and a tie-out cable. Neil hooked one end of the cable to a post in the ground. He clipped the other end to Moose's collar. *He's big,* Neil thought. *But that should hold him.*

Moose sat and waited until Neil went inside. Then he turned his head and looked all around. Convinced no one was watching, he jumped up, raced to the end of his run, and lunged.

Crack! The clasp on his collar snapped. The collar fell off his neck. And Moose bounded away as if he had busted out of jail.

Neil bought collar after collar, each one stronger than the last. Moose broke them all. Once he even snapped off the metal hook on the end of his cable. Moose never wandered far, and he always came home. But his escapes worried Neil. "This dog would never hurt anyone on purpose," he told Aline, "but he doesn't know his own strength."

Moose peels, er, pulls a fast one. The banana-loving mutt snatched this treat off a neighbor's table.

Chapter 2

NOTHING BUT TROUBLE

One month after finding Moose, Aline took him outside. She clipped the tie-out cable to his collar and threw a toy for him. But the excited puppy didn't chase it. He ran around Aline instead, looping his cable around her legs. Aline scrambled to get loose. But she had freed only one leg before the loop tightened.

"Moose, no!" she screamed.

Too late. Moose yanked her off her feet, and snap! The cable broke her ankle in four places.

Neil blamed himself. He had kept Moose despite his fear that something bad might happen. Now it had!

Aline needed surgery. The doctor used seven pins, two screws, and a metal plate to fix her ankle. He put her foot and lower leg in a cast and sent her home on crutches.

Now Neil had another reason to worry. *What if Moose jumped on Aline when she was hobbling about?* To protect her, Neil boarded Moose at a local vet clinic. Later he took the pup to stay with Tony Segee (sounds like SEG-ee). Tony was a professional dog trainer. He would teach Moose to obey simple commands.

And Moose was easy to train, except for one thing. "Moose is too interested in other dogs," Tony said. Still, Tony taught him to come when called and not to jump on people.

After a couple of months, Aline's bones had healed. She still needed physical therapy (sounds like FIZ-uh-kul THER-uh-pee) to build up her muscles. But Moose could come home! He burst into the house with his tail wagging. He was so happy to be back.

Since her injury, Aline hated the tie-out cable. It made her nervous. So Neil replaced it with a 50-foot (15-m) nylon leash he hooked to the post in the ground. But now Moose began chewing through the leash to escape!

Picking a Pup

Dogs come in almost 400 breeds. People trust dog breeders to only mate a beagle with a beagle or a poodle with a poodle. That way, if you buy a purebred dog, you know what you're getting.

But maybe you aren't that fussy. Then you can visit an animal shelter and take home a mutt. Mutts are mixed breeds, like Moose. They come in all sizes, shapes, colors, and patterns. No one can predict how they will behave. But one thing is for sure. Mutts can make wonderful pets.

The dog was also having weird spells. They started with him standing still and swallowing hard. Then he ran from room to room licking the floor. Each spell lasted for hours.

One day Moose stopped eating. Aline called Dr. Fuller. "He probably ate something he shouldn't have," the vet said. "Feed him chicken broth and rice."

They did, but the next morning Moose threw up. Not food. Pieces of his tie-out leash! "I kept knotting it back together," Neil said. "I didn't realize he was eating it!"

Aline called Dr. Fuller again. "Bring him in!" said the vet. She gave Moose fluids and watched him closely. Two days later she called. "Moose can go home on Monday," she told Aline.

But Monday morning, Dr. Fuller called again. "Moose ate his blanket and is throwing up. We have to keep him."

When Moose was finally released, the vet was concerned. "He can't keep eating this stuff," she said. "You better muzzle him." She showed Neil a wire cage that fit over Moose's mouth.

Neil hated the thought. But Moose had escaped too many times. He had chowed down too many wrong things. Neil and Aline had to do something. "We'll think about it," Neil said.

The next morning, Aline awoke to the sound of Moose throwing up. She found piles of slimy brown blanket on the floor. Plus, Moose had thrown up five more pieces of leash. One piece measured almost a yard (0.9 m) long! It had been in his stomach for over three weeks. "Unbelievable!" said Dr. Fuller.

Moose ate socks, pajama bottoms, and a lightbulb next. "This dog is nothing but trouble," Neil groaned.

Yet the goofy mutt wasn't all bad. Tony had trained him to always wait at the door and let Aline go through first. But once she forgot to give the commands. Moose sprinted past her and into the house. Then he skidded to a stop, raced back, and sat. He corrected himself!

Did You Know?

Dirty socks are the number one nonfood item eaten by dogs.

Another time, Moose stole a slipper. Neil chased the playful pup and got it back. But he couldn't find its mate.

"Where's the other one?" he sputtered, searching for it. Moose cocked his head. Then he disappeared. Minutes later he dropped the missing slipper at Neil's feet and wagged his tail. He seemed to say, *See? I can be good.*

The trouble was that every time Moose did something good, he followed with something bad. Twice he chased a skunk and stunk up the house. Another time he stole a whole loaf of bread—from a neighbor's kitchen.

That June, Aline finished physical therapy. She could walk normally again. But she feared being around Moose when he was tied up.

Did You Know?

Scientists say dogs are four times more likely to steal food when they think you're not looking.

So she and Neil let the pup run loose outside and tried to train him to stay close to home. But the minute no one was watching, he sneaked away to visit the neighbor's pooch.

One day, Neil was Moose-sitting and got distracted. Aline came home from shopping to find three teenagers leading Moose away. One of the teenagers was using his belt as a leash. "We found him in the road," they explained. "We thought he was lost."

Moose had broken his own collar and was wearing a hand-me-down collar bearing another dog's name. Now Neil ordered him a new one—with Moose's name and Aline's cell phone number printed on it. It came just in time.

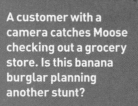

A customer with a camera catches Moose checking out a grocery store. Is this banana burglar planning another stunt?

Chapter 3

MOOSE ON THE LOOSE

Moose was wearing his new collar when Aline's phone rang. "This is the state police," a man said. "A woman found your dog and brought him here."

Not again! Moose had been gone such a short time, no one had even noticed him missing!

Just as Moose loved sneaking away, he enjoyed using his head to solve problems. One time, just for fun, Neil tied one of Moose's tennis balls up in a tree. He used a slipknot to hold it in place. That way the ball would come loose if Moose pulled the long end of the rope. But Moose kept trying to knock the ball down with his paws. Finally, Aline pretended to grab the rope with her mouth. Moose watched her. Then he gripped the rope with his teeth, pulled, and the ball fell down!

Despite the fun, Moose still got sick a lot. One day Aline took him to the vet to get a sore on his neck checked out. Dr. Jennifer Niedziela (sounds like NAH-jel-ah) was on duty that day. She said the sore was a "hot spot" caused by a food allergy. She said that Moose shouldn't eat wheat, dairy, chicken, or beef. "Okay,"

Aline said. "But, while he's here, please x-ray his stomach."

The vet was surprised. "Why?"

Aline told her about the many spells of gulping, pacing, and floor licking Moose had had.

The x-ray showed nothing. But Dr. Niedziela kept looking for a cause for the strange spells. She talked with the other vets who had treated Moose. Together, they decided on a new diagnosis (sounds like di-ag-NO-sis): acid reflux (sounds like REE-flucks). This meant partly digested food was bubbling out of his stomach and pushing back up through the tube to his throat. People can get acid reflux, too.

This condition made Moose feel like throwing up. Then he licked and ate anything he could find, trying to make that sick feeling go away.

Vets had given Moose acid reflux pills before, but nothing helped. His case was too severe. Now Dr. Niedziela said to give him the same strong medicine that people take for acid reflux. That worked! Moose's weird spells stopped. So did most of his crazy eating.

Two years had passed since the Newmans found Moose. Aline's ankle had healed and she had taken over the dog walking from Neil. But one day she skipped their walk. Moose got restless. That evening he kept nudging her elbow. "Oh, okay," groaned Aline, and she got to

Did You Know?

Most human medicines are too strong or dangerous for pets. Always talk to your vet before giving your pet medicine!

her feet. They had walked about a mile, when two whitetail deer suddenly appeared. Fearing a showdown, Aline hurried Moose across the road.

Big mistake! She and Moose had plunged straight into a larger group of deer, which were grazing in the shadows! Moose's tail shot up. He perked his ears. The deer lifted their heads and stared at them. Aline sucked in her breath. *Deer sometimes attack dogs,* she thought. *Could Moose and I get stomped to death?*

Moose also sensed danger. Stepping between Aline and the whitetails, he quickly sat down. For several minutes he sat without moving. His message was clear: *Don't worry. I mean no harm.* One by one, the deer relaxed.

People vs. Pups

Dogs are so much like us. They follow us around, live in our homes, and sometimes eat the same food. They even feel the same joy, hope, sadness, and fear that we do. But dogs aren't human. Here are some of the ways we differ:

	HUMANS	DOGS
Number of Scent Cells in Nose	6 million	300 million
Number of Teeth	32	42
Number of Eyelids	2	3
Number of Bones	206	320
Average Number of Words Understood	60,000	165
Tallest	8 feet, 11 inches (2.72 m)	3 feet, 8 inches (1.12 m)
Average Life Span	71 years	10–12 years

They went back to eating. Aline whispered thanks as she and Moose quietly slipped away.

Moose's behavior had certainly improved. But his sense of adventure remained. That December, Neil and Aline decided to go shopping. As they prepared to leave the house, Moose sat by the door thumping his tail. His eyes shone bright with hope. Neil sighed. "Okay," he told the dog. "You can come."

At the store, the parking lot was crowded. They had to park far from the entrance. "Stay," Neil told Moose. "It could get too hot inside this van in summer. But it's cold today, so you'll be fine." Neil and Aline got out, and Neil shut the door. He clicked his remote.

Beep! The doors were locked.

The Newmans went to frozen foods first. From there, Neil led the way to the pet department. He wanted to buy Moose a new toy. They were checking out chew toys when Aline's cell phone rang. She didn't recognize the number.

"Do you own a dog named Moose?" a woman asked.

"Yes," said Aline, her mind racing.

"Well," said the caller, "he's here in the store, over by frozen foods!"

In the store? Dumbfounded, Aline started running.

"Where are you going?" Neil yelled.

"To get Moose! Moose is in the store!" she hollered back.

"He can't be," Neil said. "It must be some kind of joke."

Nope. Aline kept going and sure enough, there was Moose. He was sitting in the same spot she and Neil had left only moments before. Amused shoppers stood all around him.

The store had automatic doors, so it was no mystery how Moose got inside. But how did he get out of the van? Did some stranger use a car remote whose frequency matched theirs? Or did Moose open the door himself by pushing the button with his nose?

Aline and Neil will never know.

But they do know this. When it really mattered, Moose did not run off in search of other dogs. He went looking for his human family. Neil and Aline are almost as glad of that as they are of finding Moose in the first place. "Sometimes I get so mad at him," Neil says. "But there's so much love in his eyes that I can't stay angry."

Mostly Neil just shrugs his shoulders, shakes his head, and laughs.

THE END

Guess what? Aline Alexander Newman is not only the author of this book, she also took part in this story! Aline and her husband, Neil, adopted Moose in 2012.

DON'T MISS!

NATIONAL GEOGRAPHIC KiDS   **CHAPTERS**

HOOPS TO HIPPOS!

True Stories of a
Basketball Star
on Safari!

NBA Player Boris Diaw
With Kitson Jazynka

**Turn the page
for a sneak preview . . .**

That's me, Boris Diaw. Two of my favorite things are playing hoops and taking photos of wild animals. I photographed these hippos when I was in Africa on safari, a special trip to see wildlife.

HOOPS TO HIPPOS!

I loved watching this little lion cub lounge on a termite mound.

THE WILD LIFE

Hi, my name is Boris Diaw (sounds like DEE-ow). I'm a professional basketball player. I play for the National Basketball Association, or NBA, for short. I play all over the United States. I also play in Europe.

I have played hoops my whole life. I grew up in a small town named Bordeaux (sounds like bore-DOH) in southwest France.

My mom was a pro basketball player, too. She used to shoot hoops with me. The game was her passion. Now it's mine, too.

I love how basketball is a team sport. There's a lot of spirit in it. Everyone on a team must work together. It's like a pride of lions or a pack of African wild dogs.

Animals are another passion of mine. I love spending time outdoors and taking pictures of wild animals. I have taken photographs of wildlife in South Africa, Botswana (sounds like bot-SWAN-uh), Tanzania (sounds like tan-zan-EE-yuh), and India. I've watched hungry lions eat. I've tracked a tigress with her cubs. I have photographed colorful birds, rugged rhinos, and lounging leopards. When I'm at home in San Antonio, Texas, U.S.A., my photos remind me of the peace I feel in the wild.

I started taking pictures of wildlife when I was seven years old. I was on a trip with my mom and my brother, Martin. We had gone to Senegal (sounds like sen-ih-GAWL) to visit my father. Senegal is a small country on the west coast of Africa. My dad still lives there today, in a city named Dakar (sounds like dah-CAR).

Martin and I had never been to Africa before. It was a big adventure for us. Dakar was very different from where we lived. The city smelled musty. The food tasted spicy.

During the trip, I got a disposable camera. I liked taking pictures of Dakar and all the people around me. But what I really wanted to see and photograph were wild animals.

Lion Tracking

Many wildlife lovers on safari hope to see lions. Trackers help find lions by looking for clues in the bush. They look for paw prints or signs of a kill, such as an animal's hide on the ground or bones. They listen for the roar of lions and calls of alarm from animals that lions like to eat. They sniff the air for the sharp smell of lion scat, or poop. Following clues from the bush just might lead to an awesome encounter with a big cat—just don't get too close!

I was excited when we went to camp in the Niokolo-Koba (sounds like NYUH-koh-loh KOH-ba) National Park. My dad told us we'd see wild animals there. It felt like the longest drive ever—eight hours! As we drove deeper into Africa, it got hotter. We weren't far from the Sahara. It was hotter than any place I knew. There were also lots of big, biting flies.

At the wildlife park, we saw hippos, monkeys, and antelope. We saw zebras and giraffes, too. I watched warthogs and their babies. They trotted around with tails held high. We watched and listened to birds, such as parrots and bee-eaters.

Wild animals here seemed different …

Want to know what happens next? Be sure to check out _Hoops to Hippos!_

INDEX

MORE INFORMATION

To find more information about the animal species featured in this book, check out these books, magazine articles, websites, and videos:

Animal Planet Rabbits, Animal Planet Pet Care Library, 2015.

How to Speak Dog: A Guide to Decoding Dog Language, by Aline Alexander Newman and Gary Weitzman, National Geographic, 2013.

National Geographic Kids Everything Dogs, by Becky Baines, National Geographic, 2012.

House Rabbit Network
www.rabbitnetwork.org

National Geographic "Animals: Domestic Dogs"
animals.nationalgeographic.com/animals/mammals/
domestic-dog

National Geographic "Spirit Bear"
ngm.nationalgeographic.com/2011/08/kermode-bear/
barcott-text

National Geographic Wild Detectives: Bear Bandits
video.nationalgeographic.com/video/wd-ep8-bearbandits

Bugs (on the cover) shown here as a very fluffy baby

This book of funny stories is dedicated to my granddaughter, Maya Rae, who is always smiling.
—A. A. N.

CREDITS

Cover, Callie Broaddus; 4–5, Callie Broaddus; 6, Aline Alexander Newman; 10, pengpeng/iStockphoto; 16, Callie Broaddus; 21, wavebreakmedia/Shutterstock; 26, Callie Broaddus; 35, Callie Broaddus; 36–37, Design Pics Inc/Alamy; 38, Chris Wallace/Alamy; 43, Sumio Harada/Minden Pictures; 48, Benjamin P. Tabor; 57, BearVault; 58, Donald M. Jones/Minden Pictures/Corbis; 63, Bucks Wildlife Photography/Getty Images; 68–69, Aline Alexander Newman; 70, Aline Alexander Newman; 77, Robert Daly/Getty Images; 80, Aline Alexander Newman; 84, PK-Photos/iStockphoto; 90, Aline Alexander Newman; 96, Arthur Tilley/Getty Images; 102 (LO LE), Hugues Lawson-Body; 102–103, Boris Diaw; 104, Boris Diaw; 108, Boris Diaw; 111, Callie Broaddus

ACKNOWLEDGMENTS

A special thanks to:

My husband, Neil, for loving Moose—and me.

Our younger son, Wade, for agreeing to be interviewed and making several helpful suggestions.

Benjamin P. Tabor, NYSDEC wildlife biologist, who spent an entire day with me and answered countless follow-up questions.

Callie Broaddus, associate designer at National Geographic Children's Books, for sharing her tales of animal life at Tranquility Post.

Marfé Ferguson Delano, freelance project editor for National Geographic Children's Books, for all expert assistance and good ideas.

Shelby Alinsky, Bri Bertoia, and the rest of the National Geographic staff for producing a finished book that makes me proud.

About the author: www.alinealexandernewman.com